# HSP Science

# Teaching Resources
## Grade 3

 Harcourt
SCHOOL PUBLISHERS

*Visit The Learning Site!*
**www.harcourtschool.com**

# Contents

### Dear Family,

In science class, we will be using HSP SCIENCE by *Harcourt School Publishers*. This textbook program provides comprehensive science content and hands-on experiences, and it offers interesting facts, concepts, and graphics. The graphics help create exciting pages and enable students to grasp information through visual cues.

There are many ways you can help your child with science this year. Here are some ideas:

- Encourage your child to read science library books about topics related to the units and chapters he or she is studying.

- Work with your child to do science projects that are suggested in the HSP SCIENCE program.

- Discuss with your child science news stories that you hear in media reports. Use science vocabulary words from the textbook chapters when you discuss the stories.

- With your child, visit your public library or use Internet resources to research chapter topics and to find additional information. Find out about recent discoveries in science and how they affect your daily life.

- Visit **www.hspscience.com** for more activities and resources.

Sincerely,

## Queridos familiares,

En la clase de Ciencias usaremos el libro de texto HSP SCIENCE de *Harcourt School Publishers*. Este programa contiene información científica integral y experimentos, así como datos, conceptos y gráficas interesantes. Las gráficas ayudan a que las páginas resulten más atractivas y sirven como ayudas visuales para que el estudiante capte la información de una manera más efectiva.

Este año, para la clase de Ciencias, ustedes pueden ayudar a su niño de muchas maneras. Estas son algunas ideas:

- Animen al niño a leer libros de Ciencias de la biblioteca que estén relacionados con las unidades y capítulos en estudio.

- Hagan juntos los proyectos que se mencionan en el programa HSP SCIENCE.

- Hablen acerca de noticias científicas que hayan escuchado recientemente. Usen palabras del vocabulario de Ciencias.

- Vayan a la biblioteca pública o usen Internet para investigar y obtener información adicional acerca de los temas de estudio del capítulo. Busquen datos sobre descubrimientos recientes que muestren que las Ciencias son una parte fascinante de la vida diaria.

- Visiten **www.hspscience.com** para obtener más actividades y sugerencias.

Atentamente,

# School-Home Connection
### Life Science, Units A and B

## Dear Family,

We are doing hands-on investigations in our science class. To do the investigations in our life science chapters, we will need some materials that you may have around the home. Please note the items below. If possible, please send these things to school with your child. Your help and support are appreciated.

Sincerely,

<table>
<tr><td colspan="2" align="center">Materials List</td></tr>
<tr><td>

_____ aquarium gravel  
_____ chenille sticks, white (12")  
_____ construction paper  
_____ crayons  
_____ glue  
_____ grass (plant)  
_____ index cards  
_____ jar with lid (1-L)  
_____ large plastic bowl  
_____ latex gloves  
_____ lima bean seeds  
_____ oatmeal  
_____ paper and pencils  
_____ paper cups (200 mL)  
_____ paper towels  
_____ permanent marker  
_____ plastic spoons  

</td><td>

_____ poster board  
_____ potting soil  
_____ red yarn  
_____ shoe box  
_____ small plant  
_____ spray bottle with trigger  
_____ square piece of dark felt  
_____ transparent tape  
_____ vegetable shortening  
_____ watering can  
_____ white paper  
_____ wire clothes hanger  
_____ zip-top plastic bag (3" × 4")  
_____ _______________________  
_____ _______________________  
_____ _______________________  
_____ _______________________  

</td></tr>
</table>

## Queridos familiares,

En nuestra clase de Ciencias estamos realizando diferentes experimentos. Para las investigaciones que corresponden a los capítulos de Ciencias Biológicas necesitaremos algunos materiales que tal vez tengan en su casa. Por favor miren la lista de abajo. Si es posible, manden con su hijo los materiales que tengan disponibles. Les agradecemos la ayuda y el apoyo que nos brinden.

Atentamente,

<table>
<tr><td colspan="2" align="center">Materiales</td></tr>
<tr><td>

_____ grava para acuario
_____ limpiapipas blancos (12")
_____ cartulina
_____ crayolas
_____ pegamento
_____ pasto (planta)
_____ tarjetas
_____ frasco con tapa (1-L)
_____ tazón grande de plástico
_____ guantes de látex
_____ habas
_____ avena
_____ papel y lápices
_____ vasos de cartón (200 mL)
_____ toallas de papel
_____ marcador permanente
_____ cucharas de plástico

</td><td>

_____ cartulina grande
_____ tierra para macetas
_____ estambre rojo
_____ caja de zapatos
_____ planta pequeña
_____ botella rociadora
_____ cuadrado de fieltro oscuro
_____ cinta adhesiva transparente
_____ manteca vegetal
_____ regadera
_____ papel blanco
_____ gancho de ropa metálico
_____ bolsa de plástico con cierre (3" × 4")
_____ _______________________
_____ _______________________
_____ _______________________

</td></tr>
</table>

## Dear Family,

We are doing hands-on investigations in our science class. To do the investigations in our earth science chapters, we will need some materials that you may have around the home. Please note the items below. If possible, please send these things to school with your child. Your help and support are appreciated.

Sincerely,

---

### Materials List

| | |
|---|---|
| _____ aluminum pan | _____ paper cups (200 mL) |
| _____ baking soda | _____ paper plates (9") |
| _____ ballpoint pen cap | _____ paper towels |
| _____ bathroom scale | _____ pencils |
| _____ black and red markers | _____ petroleum jelly |
| _____ cardboard strips | _____ plastic spoons |
| _____ clear plastic cups | _____ plastic/inflatable globe |
| _____ colored pencils | _____ potting soil |
| _____ D-cell battery | _____ round toothpicks |
| _____ deli-type container | _____ seashells |
| _____ flashlight | _____ spray bottle with trigger |
| _____ flour (I lb) | _____ transparent tape |
| _____ food coloring (set of 4) | _____ trash bag |
| _____ glue | _____ used, washed aluminum cans |
| _____ graph paper | _____ vegetable oil |
| _____ gravel | _____ vinegar |
| _____ measuring cup | _____ volleyball |
| _____ measuring spoons | _____ wax paper |
| _____ non-iodized salt | _____ wide-mouth specimen jar with lid (237 mL) |
| _____ oatmeal-raisin cookies | _____ ________________________ |
| _____ opaque plastic cups (300 mL) | _____ ________________________ |
| _____ paper | |

## Queridos familiares,

En nuestra clase de Ciencias estamos realizando diferentes experimentos. Para las investigaciones que corresponden a los capítulos de Ciencias de la Tierra necesitaremos algunos materiales que tal vez tengan en su casa. Por favor miren la lista de abajo. Si es posible, manden con su hijo los materiales que tengan disponibles. Les agradecemos la ayuda y el apoyo que nos brinden.

Atentamente,

---

### Materiales

| | |
|---|---|
| _____ molde de aluminio | _____ vasos de cartón (200 mL) |
| _____ bicarbonato de sodio | _____ platos de cartón (9") |
| _____ tapa de bolígrafo | _____ toallas de papel |
| _____ báscula de baño | _____ lápices |
| _____ marcadores negros y rojos | _____ vaselina |
| _____ tiras de cartón | _____ cucharas de plástico |
| _____ vasos de plástico transparente | _____ globo terráqueo de plástico/ inflable |
| _____ lápices de colores | _____ tierra para macetas |
| _____ pila tamaño D | _____ mondadientes redondos |
| _____ recipiente reciclable del delicatessen | _____ conchitas de mar |
| _____ linterna | _____ botella rociadora |
| _____ harina (I lb) | _____ cinta adhesiva transparente |
| _____ colorante para alimentos (caja de 4) | _____ bolsa de basura |
| _____ pegamento | _____ latas de aluminio usadas y limpias |
| _____ papel para gráficas | _____ aceite vegetal |
| _____ grava | _____ vinagre |
| _____ taza para medir | _____ voleibol |
| _____ cucharas para medir | _____ papel encerado |
| _____ sal no yodada | _____ frasco de boca ancha para muestras, con tapa (237 mL) |
| _____ galletas de avena y pasas | _____ ________________________ |
| _____ vasos de plástico opaco (300 mL) | _____ ________________________ |
| _____ papel | |

## Dear Family,

We are doing hands-on investigations in our science class. To do the investigations in our physical science chapters, we will need some materials that you may have around the home. Please note the items below. If possible, please send these things to school with your child. Your help and support are appreciated.

Sincerely,

---

### Materials List

| | |
|---|---|
| _____ brown rice | _____ piece of wool cloth (12" × 24") |
| _____ cardboard tubes | _____ pinto bean seeds |
| _____ checkerboard | _____ plastic beads |
| _____ checkers | _____ plastic bowl (20 oz) |
| _____ clear plastic cups (300 mL) | _____ plastic comb |
| _____ coins | _____ plastic jar |
| _____ cookie sheet | _____ plastic lid |
| _____ crayons | _____ plastic slinky |
| _____ D-cell battery | _____ plastic spoons |
| _____ flashlight | _____ plastic straws |
| _____ flat eraser | _____ poster board |
| _____ jump rope | _____ pushpins |
| _____ masking tape | _____ red food coloring |
| _____ measuring cup | _____ string |
| _____ measuring spoons | _____ tape measure |
| _____ metal buttons | _____ toy cars (pull-back action) |
| _____ metal teaspoon | _____ toy truck (matchbox-type) |
| _____ non-iodized salt | _____ white rice |
| _____ paper (red and white) | _____ _______________________ |
| _____ paper clips | _____ _______________________ |
| _____ pencils with eraser | _____ _______________________ |
| _____ penny | _____ _______________________ |

## Queridos familiares,

En nuestra clase de Ciencias estamos realizando diferentes experimentos. Para las investigaciones que corresponden a los capítulos de Ciencias Físicas necesitaremos algunos materiales que tal vez tengan en su casa. Por favor miren la lista de abajo. Si es posible, manden con su hijo los materiales que tengan disponibles. Les agradecemos la ayuda y el apoyo que nos brinden.

Atentamente,

<table>
<tr><td colspan="2" align="center">Materiales</td></tr>
<tr><td>_____ arroz integral</td><td>_____ pedazo de lana (12" × 24")</td></tr>
<tr><td>_____ tubos de cartón</td><td>_____ frijoles pintos</td></tr>
<tr><td>_____ tablero de juego de damas</td><td>_____ cuentas de plástico</td></tr>
<tr><td>_____ juego de damas</td><td>_____ tazón de plástico (20 oz)</td></tr>
<tr><td>_____ vaso de plástico transparente (300 mL)</td><td>_____ peine de plástico</td></tr>
<tr><td>_____ monedas</td><td>_____ frasco de plástico</td></tr>
<tr><td>_____ bandeja para hornear galletas</td><td>_____ tapa de plástico</td></tr>
<tr><td>_____ crayolas</td><td>_____ slinky de plástico</td></tr>
<tr><td>_____ pila tamaño D</td><td>_____ cucharas de plástico</td></tr>
<tr><td>_____ linterna</td><td>_____ pajitas de plástico</td></tr>
<tr><td>_____ goma de borrar plana</td><td>_____ cartulina grande</td></tr>
<tr><td>_____ cuerda para saltar</td><td>_____ tachuelas</td></tr>
<tr><td>_____ cinta de enmascarar</td><td>_____ colorante rojo para alimentos</td></tr>
<tr><td>_____ taza de medir</td><td>_____ hilo</td></tr>
<tr><td>_____ cucharas de medir</td><td>_____ cinta métrica</td></tr>
<tr><td>_____ botones metálicos</td><td>_____ carros de juguete (de fricción)</td></tr>
<tr><td>_____ cuchara metálica para té</td><td>_____ camioneta de juguete (miniatura)</td></tr>
<tr><td>_____ sal no yodada</td><td>_____ arroz blanco</td></tr>
<tr><td>_____ papel (rojo y blanco)</td><td>_____ _______________________</td></tr>
<tr><td>_____ clips</td><td>_____ _______________________</td></tr>
<tr><td>_____ lápices con borrador</td><td>_____ _______________________</td></tr>
<tr><td>_____ moneda de 1¢</td><td></td></tr>
</table>

### Dear Family,

In the next few weeks, we will be learning about these topics in science class:

Here are some of the vocabulary terms we will be learning:

You can help me at home by reminding me to use these terms when we are talking.

We can also read science library books together and complete science projects.

Sincerely,



---

**Teachers**—The above is a note that students can complete and take home. Have students fill in chapter topics and vocabulary. For home activities, have students also take home a copy of the chapter's Science Projects for Home or School (pages TR11–TR26).

## Queridos familiares,

Durante las próximas semanas, estaremos estudiando los siguientes temas en la clase de Ciencias:

Estas son algunas palabras del vocabulario que estaremos aprendiendo:

Ayúdenme a recordar estas palabras y a usarlas en nuestras conversaciones.

También podemos leer libros de la biblioteca y realizar proyectos de Ciencias juntos.

Atentamente,



---

**Maestros: Esta es una nota que los alumnos pueden completar y llevar a casa. Pídales que anoten los temas y el vocabulario del capítulo. Para actividades de la casa, pida que también se lleven una copia del proyecto de Ciencias del capítulo (Science Projects for Home or School) (páginas TR11–TR26).**

# You Can Do It!

## Quick and Easy Project

### Frog Life Cycle

**Procedure**

1. Look up the stages in the life cycle of a frog.
2. As the tadpole develops into a frog, what things about it change?
3. Draw each stage of a frog's life cycle.
4. Cut out and arrange your drawings in a shoe box decorated to look like a place where a frog lives.

**Materials**

- construction paper
- crayons or markers
- scissors
- shoe box or other cardboard box

**Draw Conclusions**

What word describes the changes that take place in a frog as it develops?

## Design Your Own Investigation

### How Do Potatoes Grow?

Find four different kinds of potatoes. Stick five toothpicks around the center of each potato. Set the toothpicks on the rim of a jar so the potato hangs into the jar. Add water to the jar, until the bottom of the potato is covered. Observe your potatoes for several days. Keep water in the jar. Record your observations.

# You Can Do It!



## A Fresh Start

### Procedure

1. **CAUTION:** Be careful when using scissors. Cut off a 15-cm piece of the plant. Make sure a stem and at least one leaf are on the cut piece.

2. Fill the bottle with water. Place the cut stem in the water. The leaf should be sticking out of the water.

3. Place the plant in a sunny spot. Check it every day. Keep the bottle filled with water.

### Materials

- 1 plant with many stems and leaves
- scissors
- ruler
- 1-L plastic bottle
- water

### Draw Conclusions

Observe the plant for ten days. Record any changes you observe.



## Growing Groceries

Think about the plants you eat. How do potatoes, pineapples, and peas grow? What parts do they have that might grow new plants? Choose from the grocery store a plant you eat. Make a prediction about how a new plant could come from it. Then plan and conduct an investigation to see if you were right.

# You Can Do It!

## Quick and Easy Project

# Goldfish Gills

### Procedure

1. Study the goldfish. Locate its gill coverings.

2. Use a stopwatch to count the number of times the gill coverings open and close in 15 seconds.

3. How could you use this number to find out how many times the goldfish opens the gill coverings in one minute?

## Materials

- goldfish in bowl with water and water plants
- stopwatch

## Draw Conclusions

Observe the goldfish for ten days. Record its gill opening rate once each day. Did the rate change? Record your data in a bar graph.

## Design Your Own Investigation

# Ready, Set, Breathe

Think about your own breathing. Predict how activity will affect your breathing rate. Then design an investigation to see if your prediction is correct.

# You Can Do It!

## Quick and Easy Project

### What Is in Soil?

**Materials**
- soil with plants
- small shovel
- hand lens
- sheet of white paper
- pencil

**Procedure**

1. Dig up a small amount of soil, including plants.

2. Put the soil on the white paper. Use the pencil to break apart the soil.

3. Use the hand lens to observe the living things you find.

4. What living things did you find? What nonliving things did you find?

**Draw Conclusions**

How do the living things in the soil interact?

## Design Your Own Investigation

### Your Ecosystem

Do research on the ecosystem you live in. How much rainfall or snowfall does it get each year? What are the average temperatures in summer and winter? What kinds of animals and plants live there? Think about different ways you can observe your ecosystem. Design an observation area for observing the animals and plants in your ecosystem. Write down your observations in a journal.

# You Can Do It!

## Quick and Easy Project

# Your Food Chain

### Procedure

1. At the top of the paper, write each food you ate for one meal.

2. Below each food, draw its source. For example, milk comes from a cow. Connect the food and source with an arrow.

3. If the source is an animal, draw the animal's food below it. Connect the animal and its food with an arrow.

## Materials

- a large sheet of paper
- pencil

### Draw Conclusions

In which direction should each arrow point to show how energy moves? What should be at the bottom of each food chain?

## Design Your Own Investigation

# Food Chains from the Sea

Do you like salmon, shrimp, or scallops? Choose your favorite fish or seafood, and predict what that animal eats. Then do some research to find out if you're correct. Make a food chain that includes that seafood and ends with you. Display your food chain on a bulletin board to share with the class.

# You Can Do It!

## Quick and Easy Project

### Minerals in Sand

**Materials**
- sand
- sheet of white paper
- hand lens
- toothpick
- mineral descriptions
- measuring spoons

#### Procedure

**1.** Spread 1 tablespoon of sand on a sheet of white paper.

**2.** Observe the colors and shapes of the sand grains by using the hand lens. Each type of mineral grain has a different color and shape.

**3.** Use the toothpick to move the grains of each kind of mineral into a separate pile.

#### Draw Conclusions

Identify all the different minerals you can. Use the descriptions your teacher gives you. Which mineral is most common?

## Design Your Own Investigation

### Fossil Models

You have learned how some different kinds of fossils were formed. Make models to show how different kinds of fossils form. Use leaves, shells, clay, syrup, and other materials to make your models. Write down the steps you used to make each model. Have someone else use your steps to make his or her own model. Compare the two models.

# You Can Do It!

## Quick and Easy Project

### Shake the Earth

**Procedure**

1. Cover the top of the gelatin with plastic wrap.

2. Use the croutons to make buildings on the gelatin.

3. Move the pan up and down and from side to side. Tap one end as you move it. Observe the movement of the gelatin.

**Materials**

- baking pan filled with gelatin
- plastic wrap
- large croutons

### Draw Conclusions

Did the movement damage your "buildings"? Record your observations. How does this model an earthquake?

## Design Your Own Investigation

### Find Changes to the Land

Look for changes that have happened quickly to the land where you live. The changes can be natural. They can also be changes caused by people. Design a way to show how the land changed. You might use before and after photos or drawings. Or you might just show the effects of the changes. Then write a description of what happened.

# You Can Do It!



## Model a Water Treatment Plant

**Materials**
- water
- bowl
- soil
- coffee filter
- empty plastic jug

### Procedure

1. Put some soil into an empty plastic jug. Fill the jug with water.
2. Close the jug tightly, and shake it until the water and soil are mixed.
3. Hold a coffee filter over a bowl while a partner slowly pours some water from the jug into the filter.
4. Observe what happens.

**Draw Conclusions**
How was the dirty water similar to polluted water? What happened when the water was poured through the filter?



## What Can't Be Recycled?

Not everything can be recycled. For example, gasoline and some kinds of plastics cannot be recycled. Do research to find out which materials can be recycled and which cannot. Make a poster that shows what you learned. Include on the poster some tips on how to sort items correctly for recycling. Present your poster to the class.

# You Can Do It!

## Quick and Easy Project

### Cloud in a Jar

**Materials**
- metal pie pan
- freezer
- glass jar without lid
- hot water
- ice cubes

**Procedure**

1. Put a pan in a freezer for an hour.
2. Just before you take out the pan, have your teacher half-fill a jar with hot water.
3. Remove the pan from the freezer, and fill it with ice cubes. Place the pan on top of the jar. Leave it there for a few minutes.

### Draw Conclusions

Observe what happens inside the jar. How is this like part of the water cycle?

## Design Your Own Investigation

### Weather Station

What is the weather like today where you live? Will the weather be different tomorrow? What will the weather be like at the end of the week? Think about the different ways you can observe the weather to answer these questions. Then design a weather station to help you record the weather. Keep records about your town's weather for at least a week.

# You Can Do It!

## Quick and Easy Project

### Sunrise, Sunset

**Procedure**

**1.** Write the name of your town on a self-stick note. Stick the note on your state on a globe.

**2.** Turn off the lights in the room. Shine a flashlight on the globe.

**3.** Slowly spin the globe counterclockwise.

**Materials**
- a small self-stick note
- globe
- flashlight

**Draw Conclusions**

What happens to the place where you put the note? What does this represent? Describe why the sun appears to move slowly across the sky from east to west during a day.

## Design Your Own Investigation

### Asteroid Impact

Asteroids are chunks of rock that orbit the sun. What do you think happens when they hit a planet or a moon? Design an investigation to find out. You might drop pebbles into a tray of corn starch and then compare the surface to the surface of the moon. Write a report describing what you found out.

# You Can Do It!

## Quick and Easy Project

### Sink or Float?

**Procedure**

1. Predict whether each object will sink or float. Record your predictions in a data table.

2. Test each object. Record the results in the data table. Were your predictions correct?

**Materials**
- water
- plastic pan
- small objects

### Draw Conclusions

From your data, which objects do you infer are less dense than water? Circle the names of these objects in your data table.

## Design Your Own Investigation

# Measuring Volume

Set a measuring cup in an empty pan. Carefully fill the cup to the brim with water. Put a small but heavy object into the cup. Some water will spill over into the pan. Pour this water into another measuring cup. The amount of water equals the volume of the object. Use this procedure to measure and compare the volumes of three small objects. Make a bar graph to share your findings.

# You Can Do It!

## Quick and Easy Project

### Leaping Coin

**Materials**
- glass bottle
- quarter
- small bowl of water

**Procedure**

1. Put the bottle in a freezer for 10–15 minutes. Next dip the mouth part of the bottle in the water.

2. Wet the quarter by dipping it into the water. Put the quarter over the bottle's mouth.

3. Put your hands around the sides of the bottle, and keep them still. Record your observations.

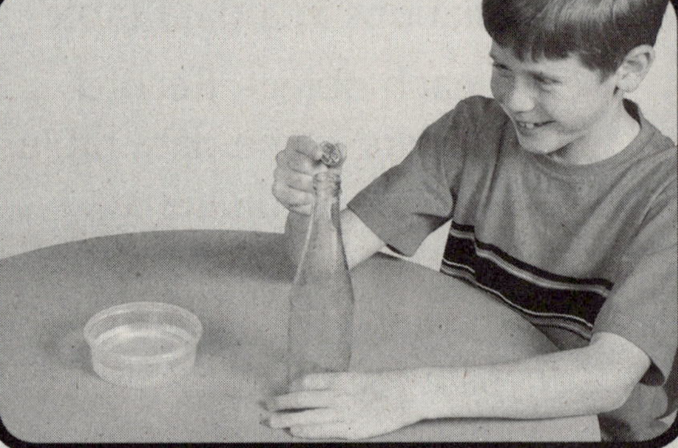

**Draw Conclusions**

Why do you think this happened to the quarter?

## Design Your Own Investigation

### Learn About Solar Energy

What is solar energy? How can you measure it? Can you build a device that uses solar energy for power? Design one or more investigations that will help you find out more about solar energy. Then gather the materials you need, and carry out your investigations.

# You Can Do It!

## Quick and Easy Project

**Materials**
- string
- ruler
- magnet
- paper
- steel paper clips

### Make a Magnetic Fishing Game

**Procedure**

**1.** Make a "fishing pole" by tying string to one end of a ruler. Tie a magnet to the other end of the string.

**2.** Cut fish shapes from paper. Tape steel paper clips to some.

**3.** Play the fishing game. Which fish can't you catch?

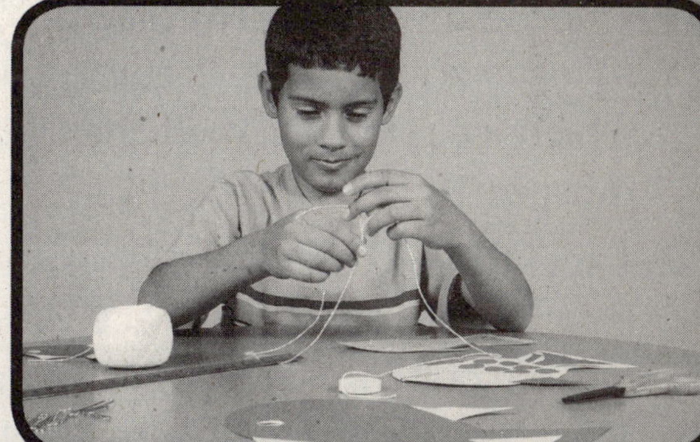

### Draw Conclusions

How can you make the fishing game work better? Predict ways to improve the design. Test your predictions.

## Design Your Own Investigation

### Static Electricity

Build up static electricity by rubbing a wool cloth over a hard rubber comb for a minute. Turn out the lights in the room. Touch the comb to a light bulb that hasn't been used in the last hour and that isn't plugged in. What happens? Repeat the procedure, touching the comb to different parts of the light bulb. Are your results different?

# You Can Do It!

## Quick and Easy Project

### Melt Down

**Procedure**

1. Choose three different places to leave an ice cube. Predict which ice cube will melt the most in 10 minutes.

2. Label three cups with the locations you will use. Place one ice cube in each cup.

3. Place the cups in their locations. After 10 minutes, observe the ice cubes.

**Materials**

- 3 ice cubes of equal size
- 3 foam cups

### Draw Conclusions

Which ice cube melted the most? Was your prediction correct? What can you conclude from your observations?

## Design Your Own Investigation

### Changing Colors

Some materials look different colors under different kinds of light. Make a list of kinds of light around your home. Don't forget streetlights or other outdoor lights. Design an experiment to see how light sources affect the colors you see. Use something with many colors, such as a brightly patterned shirt or gift-wrap paper.

# You Can Do It!

## Quick and Easy Project

## Net Force

### Procedure

1. Lay a book on a table or on the floor. Push on one side of the book. How does the book move?

2. Push on the side next to the side you just pushed. How does the book move?

3. Push on both of these sides at the same time. In which direction does the book move?

### Materials
• book

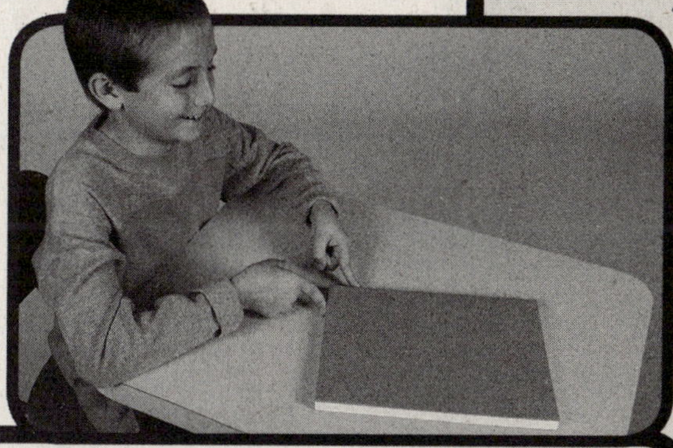

### Draw Conclusions

Why did the book move in a new direction in Step 3?

What do you think would happen if you pushed on opposite sides of the book?

## Design Your Own Investigation

## Friction

Friction is a force that you can't see. It causes objects to slow down when two surfaces rub against each other. Design an investigation to find out more about friction. Find some surfaces that are smooth and some that are rough. Then choose an object, and try moving it across the different surfaces. Do smooth surfaces or rough surfaces cause more friction?

# You Can Do It!

## Quick and Easy Project

### Making an Elevator

**Procedure**

1 Tape the pulley wheel to the underside of a box.

2 Pass the string over it.

3 Tape a paper cup to each end of the string.

4 Place pennies in one cup and then in the other. Watch your elevator move.

**Materials**
- pulley
- 2 paper cups
- string
- pennies
- tape
- box

### Draw Conclusions

How does the balance of weight affect the movement of your elevator?

## Design Your Own Investigation

### How Do Simple Machines Work?

Exactly how does a wedge work? How does a lever work? Do different levers work in different ways? How would you build a model of each of these simple machines? Sketch ideas for ways to build wedges and levers with wooden blocks. Then use your sketches as guides to build the simple machines.

# Participating in a School Science Fair

**by Barry Van Deman**

Science fairs are more than contests for students. They are events that celebrate students' interest and achievement in science. In their first few years of school, students begin to acquire science inquiry skills, such as observing, inferring, measuring, and predicting. Science projects that emphasize these skills are the most appropriate at this stage.

While individual projects at any grade level are fine, whole-class projects or small-group projects are easier to manage and give students experience in working together. In the pages that follow, this guide will focus on small-group and whole-class projects that are completed in the classroom.

The first step to ensure science fair success is to decide on the outcome you want for students and to design projects that will lead them to it. If you want your students to gain skill in observing, inferring, and classifying, you might consider having them do a project that involves collecting objects and sorting them into groups according to observable characteristics. For example, students might collect and sort leaves or observe and classify seashells. Have students record their observations in various ways, such as by drawing, by writing notes, or by making a model. These products can be part of a science project display.

The second step to science fair success is to communicate your expectations to students and to their parents or guardians. A letter you can send to parents at the start of the project is included in the following pages. Be sure to keep parents informed as the project progresses.

Finally, keep in mind that working on science fair projects can help your students gain experience in applying science inquiry skills.

## Dear Parent or Guardian,

We will be holding our school science fair on _________________.
Participating in a science fair is an enjoyable way for students to apply science inquiry skills that they have been learning at school.

Our project will focus on the following topic:

_______________________________________________

_______________________________________________

Our science fair project will emphasize the following science inquiry skill(s):

_______________________________________________

_______________________________________________

We will be doing one or more group projects at school. Your child will be part of a project team that will work on a project and display it at the science fair.

Your child can participate by:

_______________________________________________

_______________________________________________

You can aid your child's success by:

☐ helping complete research

☐ visiting _____________________________________

☐ sending in the following supplies: _____________

_______________________________________________

_______________________________________________

I will be sending home more information about our science projects and the science fair. If you have any questions, please contact me at school.

Sincerely,

**Fuzzy, Hard, and Smooth**  Have students find textures in the classroom, at home, and outdoors. Ask them to describe the textures. Groups might display labeled drawings, magazine pictures, photographs, and actual objects.

**Shapes All Around Us**  Have students find shapes in the classroom, at home, and outdoors. Ask them to identify the shapes. Groups might display labeled pictures and actual objects of various shapes.

**Sink or Float**  Have students try to float various objects in small tubs of water to see which sink and which float. Groups might display the actual objects, draw them, or show them in a table.

**All Kinds of Leaves**  Go on a leaf hunt or have students bring leaves they collect near their homes. Have students sort the leaves into groups by characteristics. They might display their groups of leaves by gluing them to poster board and labeling each group by its sorting characteristic.

**What Grows from a Seed?**  Give each student a dry bean and a paper, plastic, or foam cup filled with potting soil. Have students plant their beans just below the surface of the soil and water them thoroughly (without soaking) each day. Keep the cups near a light source, such as a window. Have students measure, draw, and record their observations daily. Groups might display their plants and charts recording their growth.

**What Will a Magnet Pick up (or Attract)?**  Give students various metallic and nonmetallic objects and a magnet. Have them test each object to find out if it is attracted to the magnet. For display, group members might draw the objects that are attracted to the magnet on one half of a sheet of poster board and objects that are not attracted on the other half.

**How Are Seashells Alike and Different?**  Have students sort a collection of seashells into groups by similar characteristics. They might display the unsorted shells along with drawings and descriptions of how they sorted them into groups.

**Which Brand of Chocolate Chip Cookies Has the Most Chocolate Chips?**  Using at least two brands of cookies, have students carefully break apart cookies and count the number of chocolate chips. Groups can collect the numbers on the chalkboard and transfer them to poster board for display. They might also want to make graphs by using "chocolate chips" made from construction paper.

For additional Science Fair project ideas, see pages in the back of the *Lab Manual*.

Here are some ideas for displaying student projects in the classroom or at a science fair.

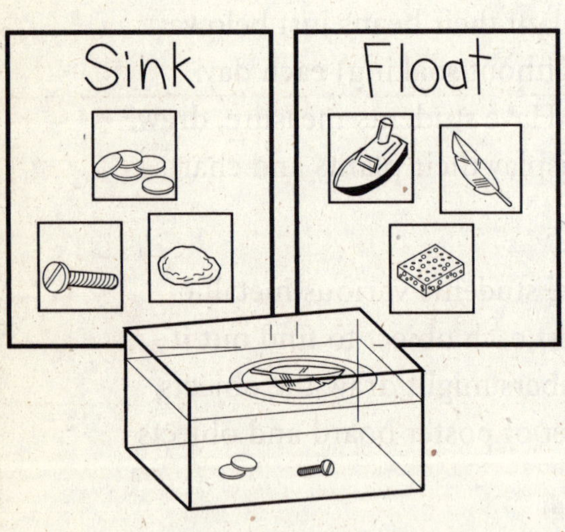


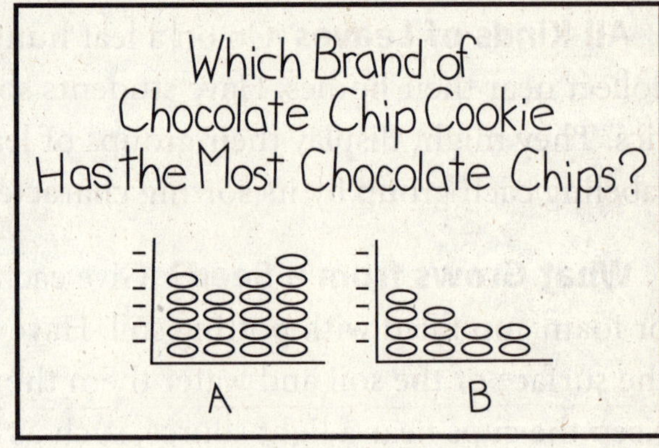

# Science Fair Project Planning

## Our Science Project Team

| Team Members | What will they do? |
| --- | --- |
|  |  |
|  |  |
|  |  |
|  |  |
|  |  |

## Project Results

## Our Project

_______________________________________________

_______________________________________________

_______________________________________________

_______________________________________________

## What We Did

_______________________________________________

_______________________________________________

_______________________________________________

_______________________________________________

## What We Found Out

_______________________________________________

_______________________________________________

_______________________________________________

_______________________________________________

# Writing Models

The writing models on the following pages show examples of writing for different purposes. Students can consult these as they complete the Writing Links in the *HSP Science* Student Edition or other writing assignments described in the Teacher Edition. You may wish to distribute copies of the writing models to students or display them on an overhead transparency.

## Informative Writing



## Persuasive Writing



## Narrative Writing



## Expressive Writing

# Writing in Science

## Model: How-To Writing

**How-to** writing gives directions or explains how to do something.
Steps are given in time order.

**topic sentence**

**materials needed**

**time-order
words in steps**

### How to Make Sun Tea

You can learn about solar radiation by making sun tea. Plan to make your tea on a warm sunny day. You need a large glass jar with a top and ten tea bags. You also need enough drinking water to fill the jar.

Start by filling the jar almost to the top with water. Add the tea bags. Then put the top on the jar. Next, place the jar in the sun. Check on your tea in two hours. You should see that the water is beginning to get darker. After four hours, taste your tea to see if it is ready. If it isn't, keep it in the sun for an hour or two longer. You may need to let your tea cool a bit before you can drink it.

You have made sun tea by using radiation from the sun!

# Writing in Science

## Model: Classification

In a **classification essay,** a writer shows how things can be grouped into categories. Often, examples of each category are provided.

| | |
|---|---|
| **title** | **Amphibians and Fish** |
| **topic sentence** | Amphibians and fish are animals that live all around us. |
| **first category defined** | Amphibians hatch from eggs that are laid in the water. They live in water when they are young. When they are older, they can move onto land. Frogs, toads, and salamanders are all amphibians. |
| **second category defined** | Fish are born in water, and most live their whole lives there. Fish use the gills on the sides of the head to breathe. They use their fins to move themselves through the water. Salmon, bass, and sharks are fish you might know. |

# Writing in Science

## Model: Research Report

A **research report** provides information about a topic. Reports can be short, or they can be several pages long.

| | |
|---|---|
| **title** | ## Owls: The Night Hunters |
| **introduction that identifies topic** | Owls are nocturnal. That means that they are most active after dark. The owl's body helps it hunt at night. |
| **body with detailed information about topic** | An owl's eyes are very large. They can see when it is almost totally dark. An owl's eyes can't move by themselves. An owl looks around by turning its head. Some owls can turn the head almost all the way around! |
| | Owls have good hearing, too. Their ears are very large. The oval shape of an owl's face helps send sound to its ears. Also, owls have very soft feathers. Their soft feathers let them fly silently and surprise their prey. |
| **conclusion** | You might be able to see an owl at the zoo. Don't miss seeing these interesting birds! |

# Writing in Science

## Model: Narration

A **narration** presents events in the order in which they occurred. Often, a narration is an eyewitness account of those events.

| | |
|---|---|
| **title** | **Water Awareness Week** |
| **topic sentence** | We had Water Awareness Week at school last week. We learned how to save water and how to keep it clean. On Monday, we learned that wasting and polluting water means less water for everyone. |
| **events described in time order** | On Tuesday and Wednesday, we studied some ways to save water. You can turn off faucets when you brush your teeth. You can take quick showers. You can let the rain water the grass. |
| | On Thursday, we made posters about saving water. We put the posters up around the school. The best part of the week was Friday. We took a class trip to our town reservoir. We learned how water gets from the reservoir to our houses. |
| **conclusion** | Water Awareness Week was fun! |

# Writing in Science

## Model: Explanation

In an **explanation,** the writer helps the reader understand something, such as what something is, how it works, what happens during a process, or why something happens.

**title**

**topic sentence**

**body/detailed explanation**

### How Sedimentary Rocks Are Formed

Sedimentary rocks are made from particles of minerals or rock. The particles are called sediment. Wind or moving water wears away the sediment from other kinds of rock. When the wind or water slows down, it drops the sediment. The sediment builds up in layers. The layers are usually on the bottom of a river, a lake, or a sea.

Over many years, the weight of the layers makes the sediment harden into rock. This rock is called sedimentary rock. After the rock is formed, wind and water can once again start to wear it away.

# Writing in Science

## Model: Compare and Contrast

In a **compare-and-contrast essay,** a writer shows how two people, places, or things are alike and how they are different.

**title** — **Venus and Mars**

**topic sentence**

**likenesses** — The planets closest to Earth are Venus and Mars. They are alike in many ways. Both are called inner planets. Inner planets are warmer than the other planets in our solar system because they are closer to the sun. Both Venus and Mars have rocky surfaces. Both planets travel around the sun in regular orbits.

**topic sentence**

**differences** — Venus and Mars are different from each other. Venus is much hotter than Mars because Venus is closer to the sun. Venus orbits the sun in about 225 Earth days. Mars's orbit takes 687 Earth days. You can see the surface of Mars from Earth, but the surface of Venus is hidden by thick clouds. Venus and Mars rotate in opposite directions. Mars has two moons, but Venus has none.

# Writing in Science

## Model: Description

A **description** creates a word picture as it tells about one subject. It has a beginning, a middle, and an ending. It includes sensory details.

| | |
|---|---|
| **title** | **The Osprey** |
| **beginning that tells what you will describe** | I walked down to the lake to fish just after five o'clock one afternoon. A few minutes later, I saw the osprey. The bird seemed to come from nowhere. It tucked its dark-colored wings tightly to its body. Then it dove toward the sparkling water. |
| **middle with sensory details** | Just before hitting the surface, the osprey opened its huge wings. It plunged its sharp claws under the water with a splash. Slowly, the bird rose from the water with a large fish grasped in its claws. I did not catch any fish |
| **ending** | myself that day. But the picture of the osprey will stay in my mind forever. |

# Writing in Science

## Model: Opinion

An **opinion** essay has a beginning, a middle with paragraphs supporting the writer's opinion, and an ending that restates the opinion or requests action.

| | |
|---|---|
| **title** | **Recycling Is Best** |
| **beginning with opinion stated** | Some people think that it's best to get rid of trash by burning it to produce energy. I think recycling is a much better idea. |
| **middle with reasons to support opinion** | Burning trash can provide energy, but it also causes air pollution. The smoke from burning trash can contain chemicals that pollute the air. If newspaper and plastic bottles are burned, new paper and plastic must be made. This causes even more pollution. |
| **ending with restated opinion or request for action** | Recycling causes less pollution than making new products. It even saves energy. That means that there will be more resources for everyone. This is why I think that recycling is better than burning trash. |

# Writing in Science

## Model: Request

To **request** information or products from a company, use a business-letter format. A business letter has the same parts as a friendly letter, plus an inside address. It also uses formal language.

| | |
|---|---|
| **heading** | 426 Harris Avenue<br>Jamaica Plain, MA 02130<br>April 8, 2009 |
| **inside address** | Ms. Nancy MacAllister<br>Broward Observatory<br>2135 Ridge Road<br>Williamstown, MA 01267 |
| **greeting** | Dear Ms. MacAllister: |
| **statement of request and supporting reasons** | Our third-grade class at Leighton Elementary School has been studying astronomy. We would like to take a tour of the Broward Observatory.<br><br>We began learning about our solar system last September. Touring the observatory would let us see how astronomers work. Using your telescope, we could get a good look at some of the planets we have been studying.<br><br>Our class can visit any time in May. Thank you for your help. |
| **closing** | Sincerely, |
| **signature** | Aaron Bishop |

© Harcourt

# Writing in Science

## Model: Business Letter

In a **business letter,** a writer uses formal language to ask for or share information, to request something, or to praise or complain about a product or service. It has the same parts as a friendly letter, plus an inside address. It also uses formal language.

| | |
|---|---|
| **heading** | 776 Main Street<br>Allegheny, NY 14706<br>September 15, 2009 |
| **inside address** | Mr. Robert B. Davies, Director<br>Wind Power Institute<br>630 Elm Street<br>Madison, WI 53706 |
| **greeting** | Dear Mr. Davies: |
| **body** | Our third-grade class at Harris Elementary School is learning about renewable energy resources. We hope that the Wind Power Institute will help us learn more about wind power.<br><br>We read about your video "Clean Power, Wind Power." I am sending a money order for $17.95 for the video. Please send it to us as soon as possible.<br><br>We are glad to have a chance to learn more about wind power. Thank you for your help. |
| **closing** | Sincerely, |
| **signature** | *Carl Olson* |

# Writing in Science

## Model: Story

Every **story** has a setting (time and place), one or more characters, and a series of events called a plot. A plot has a beginning, a middle, and an end.

| | |
|---|---|
| **title** | **The Volcano** |
| **beginning: introduce the setting and the characters** | Robert couldn't believe what he was seeing. The instruments said that the volcano was ready to erupt. There was no time to waste. |
| **middle: a plot with a problem to solve** | Robert ran to his truck and drove toward the state forest. Hundreds of people were camped there for the weekend. They had no idea that the beautiful mountain at the center of the park was about to explode.<br><br>Robert reached the forest just as the ground began to shake. He went from camp to camp, warning everyone. By then, black smoke was drifting from the mountaintop. But Robert kept the campers from panicking. At 1 P.M., the volcano erupted, destroying the |
| **end: the problem is solved** | entire state forest. But thanks to Robert, all of the campers had escaped. |

# Writing in Science

## Model: Personal Story

A **personal story** is told in the first person. Someone or something is telling the story, using pronouns such as *I*, *my*, and *me*. Like any story, a personal story has a beginning, a middle, and an end.

| | |
|---|---|
| **title** | ## My Blizzard Adventure |
| **beginning: the narrator is identified** | I have lived in San Antonio, Texas, my whole life, and I had never seen snow. I was excited to visit my cousins in Michigan for Christmas. I hoped for snow, but none fell until our last morning there. When I woke up and looked out the window, I couldn't believe my eyes! The ground was white. Huge snowflakes were falling. |
| **middle: the narrator tells a series of events** | My uncle Manny drove us to the airport to catch our flight home. Strong winds blew the snow all around. When we finally arrived, we learned that our flight wouldn't be able to leave until the storm was over. We spent twenty hours at the airport until the weather cleared. |
| **end: the narrator wraps up the story** | When we finally arrived in San Antonio, it was amazing to find hot sun and clear pavement. It was as if my adventure in the blizzard had been a dream. But I know it wasn't. I have the photos to prove it! |

# Writing in Science



A **poem** uses rhythm and language that appeals to the senses to paint a "word picture" for the reader. Some poems have rhyming lines, but some poems do not.

| | |
|---|---|
| **title** | **Hot Stuff** |
| **"word pictures" that help the reader picture what the poem is about** | To move thermal energy<br>From place to place,<br>Put a conductor<br>In the space.<br><br>To keep heat from moving,<br>Nothing is greater<br>Than filling the space<br>With an insulator. |

# Writing in Science

## Model: Friendly Letter

In a **friendly letter,** a person writes to someone he or she knows. A friendly letter has a heading, a greeting, a body, a closing, and a signature. In the heading, include one comma between the city and state and another between the day of the month and the year.

|  |  |
|---|---|
| **heading (writer's address and date)** | 412 East Houston St. San Antonio, TX 78205 May 15, 2009 |
| **greeting** | Dear Suzanne, |
| **body** | I can't wait to visit you at the farm again. Remember how much fun we had the last time? I really loved helping to harvest the vegetables. Those cucumbers were the best! This spring, my family decided to plant our own garden in the backyard. It's really tiny compared to your farm! We even started a compost pile in the backyard. Now, instead of throwing our vegetable scraps away, we compost them. Later, we'll add the compost to our garden. Maybe by the time you visit we'll have some cucumbers of our own! |
| **closing** | Your friend, |
| **signature** | Angela |

# Rubrics for Writing Practice

## A Six-Point Scoring Scale

*Student work produced for writing assessment can be scored by using a six-point scale. Although each rubric includes specific descriptors for each point score, each score can also be framed in a more global perspective.*

**SCORE OF 6: EXEMPLARY.**  Writing at this level is both exceptional and memorable. It is often characterized by distinctive and unusually sophisticated thought processes, rich details, and outstanding craftsmanship.

---

**SCORE OF 5: STRONG.**  Writing at this level exceeds the standard. It is thorough and complex, and it consistently portrays exceptional control of content and skills.

---

**SCORE OF 4: PROFICIENT.**  Writing at this level meets the standard. It is solid work that has more strengths than weaknesses. The writing demonstrates mastery of skills and reflects considerable care and commitment.

---

**SCORE OF 3: DEVELOPING.**  Writing at this level shows basic, although sometimes inconsistent, mastery and application of content and skills. It shows some strengths but tends to have more weaknesses overall.

---

**SCORE OF 2: EMERGING.**  Writing at this level is often superficial, fragmented, or incomplete. It may show a partial mastery of content and skills, but it needs considerable development before reflecting the proficient level of performance.

---

**SCORE OF 1: BEGINNING.**  Writing at this level is minimal. It typically lacks understanding and use of appropriate skills and strategies. The writing may contain major errors.

# Rubric for Ideas/Content

| Score | Description |
| --- | --- |
| 6 | The writing is exceptionally clear, focused, and interesting. It holds the reader's attention throughout. Main ideas stand out and are developed by strong support and rich details suitable to the audience and the purpose. |
| 5 | The writing is clear, focused, and interesting. It holds the reader's attention. Main ideas stand out and are developed by supporting details suitable to the audience and the purpose. |
| 4 | The writing is clear and focused. The reader can easily understand the main ideas. Support is present, although it may be limited or rather general. |
| 3 | The reader can understand the main ideas, although they may be overly broad or simplistic, and the results may not be effective. Supporting details are often limited, insubstantial, overly general, or occasionally slightly off topic. |
| 2 | The main ideas and purpose are somewhat unclear, or development is attempted but minimal. |
| 1 | The writing lacks a central idea or purpose. |

# Rubric for Organization

| Score | Description |
| --- | --- |
| 6 | The organization enhances the central idea(s) and its development. The order and structure are compelling and move the reader through the text easily. |
| 5 | The organization enhances the central idea(s) and its development. The order and structure are strong and move the reader through the text. |
| 4 | The organization is clear and coherent. Order and structure are present but may seem formulaic. |
| 3 | An attempt has been made to organize the writing; however, the overall structure is inconsistent or skeletal. |
| 2 | The writing lacks a clear organizational structure. An occasional organizational device is discernible; however, either the writing is difficult to follow and the reader has to reread substantial portions, or the piece is simply too short to demonstrate organizational skills. |
| 1 | The writing lacks coherence; organization seems haphazard and disjointed. Even after rereading, the reader remains confused. |

# Rubric for Sentence Fluency

| Score | Description |
|---|---|
| **6** | The writing has an effective flow and rhythm. Sentences show a high degree of craftsmanship, with consistently strong and varied structure that makes expressive oral reading easy and enjoyable. |
| **5** | The writing has an easy flow and rhythm. Sentences are carefully crafted, with strong and varied structure that makes expressive oral reading easy and enjoyable. |
| **4** | The writing flows; however, connections between phrases or sentences may be less than fluid. Sentence patterns are somewhat varied, contributing to ease in oral reading. |
| **3** | The writing tends to be mechanical rather than fluid. Occasional awkward constructions may force the reader to slow down or reread. |
| **2** | The writing tends to be either choppy or rambling. Awkward constructions often force the reader to slow down or reread. |
| **1** | The writing is difficult to follow or to read aloud. Sentences tend to be incomplete, rambling, or very awkward. |

# Rubric for Word Choice

| Score | Description |
|---|---|
| **6** | The words convey the intended message in an exceptionally interesting, precise, and natural way appropriate to the audience and the purpose. The writer employs a rich, broad range of words that have been carefully chosen and thoughtfully placed for impact. |
| **5** | The words convey the intended message in an interesting, precise, and natural way appropriate to the audience and the purpose. The writer employs a broad range of words that have been carefully chosen and thoughtfully placed for impact. |
| **4** | The words effectively convey the intended message. The writer employs a variety of words that are functional and appropriate to the audience and the purpose. |
| **3** | The language is quite ordinary, lacking interest, precision, and variety, or may be inappropriate to the audience and the purpose in places. The writer does not employ a variety of words, producing a sort of "generic" paper filled with familiar words and phrases. |
| **2** | The language is monotonous and/or misused, detracting from the meaning and impact. |
| **1** | The writing shows an extremely limited vocabulary or is so filled with misuses of words that the meaning is obscured. Because of vague or imprecise language, only the most general kind of message is communicated. |

# Rubric for Conventions

| Score | Description |
| --- | --- |
| 6 | The writing demonstrates exceptionally strong control of standard writing conventions (e.g., punctuation, spelling, capitalization, paragraph breaks, grammar, and usage) and uses them effectively to enhance communication. Errors are so few and so minor that the reader can easily skim right over them unless specifically searching for them. |
| 5 | The writing demonstrates strong control of standard writing conventions (e.g., punctuation, spelling, capitalization, paragraph breaks, grammar, and usage) and uses them effectively to enhance communication. Errors are so few and so minor that they do not impede readability. |
| 4 | The writing demonstrates control of standard writing conventions (e.g., punctuation, spelling, capitalization, paragraph breaks, grammar, and usage). Minor errors, while perhaps noticeable, do not impede readability. |
| 3 | The writing demonstrates limited control of standard writing conventions (e.g., punctuation, spelling, capitalization, paragraph breaks, grammar, and usage). Errors begin to impede readability. |
| 2 | The writing demonstrates little control of standard writing conventions. Frequent, significant errors impede readability. |
| 1 | Numerous errors in usage, spelling, capitalization, and punctuation repeatedly distract the reader and make the text difficult to read. In fact, the severity and frequency of errors are so overwhelming that the reader finds it difficult to focus on the message and must reread for meaning. |

# Rubric for Voice

| Score | Description |
| --- | --- |
| 6 | The writer has chosen a voice appropriate for the topic, purpose, and audience. The writer seems deeply committed to the topic, and there is an exceptional sense of "writing to be read." The writing is expressive, engaging, or sincere. |
| 5 | The writer has chosen a voice appropriate for the topic, purpose, and audience. The writer seems committed to the topic, and there is a sense of "writing to be read." The writing is expressive, engaging, or sincere. |
| 4 | A voice is present. The writer demonstrates commitment to the topic, and there may be a sense of "writing to be read." In places the writing is expressive, engaging, or sincere. |
| 3 | The writer's commitment to the topic seems inconsistent. A sense of the writer may emerge at times; however, the voice is either inappropriately personal or inappropriately impersonal. |
| 2 | The writing provides little sense of involvement or commitment. There is no evidence that the writer has chosen a suitable voice. |
| 1 | The writing seems to lack a sense of involvement or commitment. |

# Picture Sorting Cards

**Card #1**
limestone

**Card #2**
sandstone

**Card #3**
renewable resource

**Card #4**
nonrenewable resource





Picture Sorting Cards

# Picture Sorting Cards

**Card #5**
reusable resource

**Card #6**
humus

**Card #7**
sand

**Card #8**
silt

# Picture Sorting Cards

**Card #9**
clay

**Card #10**
Mercury

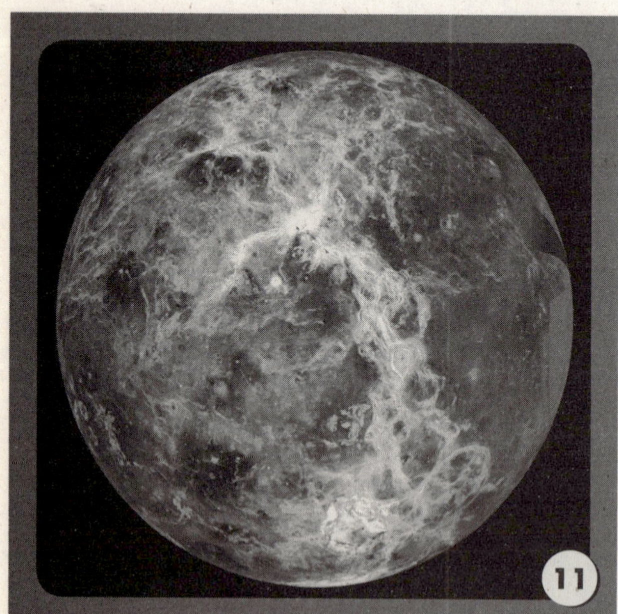

**Card #11**
Venus

**Card #12**
Earth

# Picture Sorting Cards

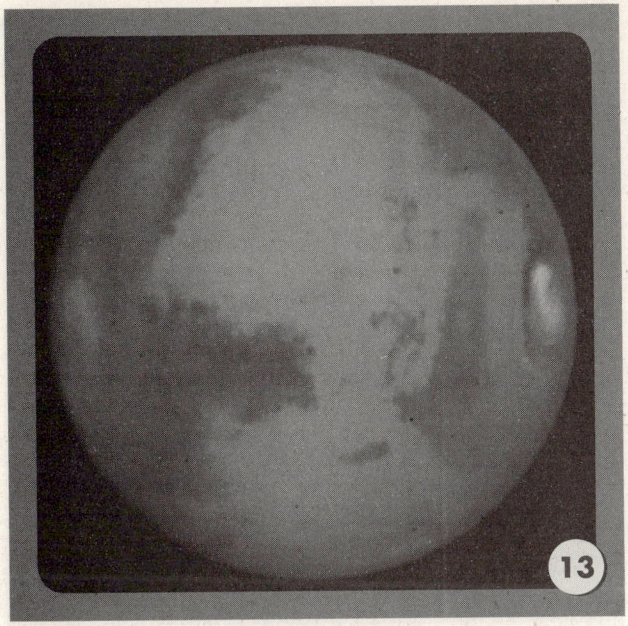

**Card #13**
Mars

**Card #14**
Jupiter

**Card #15**
Saturn

**Card #16**
Uranus

# Picture Sorting Cards

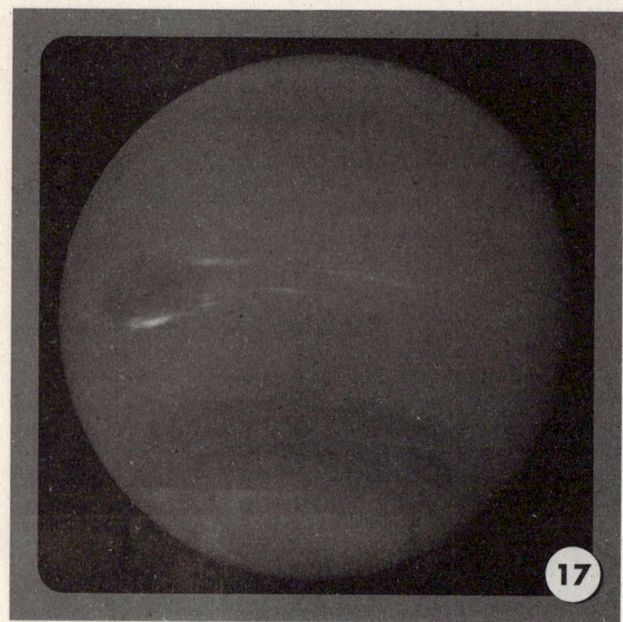

**Card #17**
Neptune

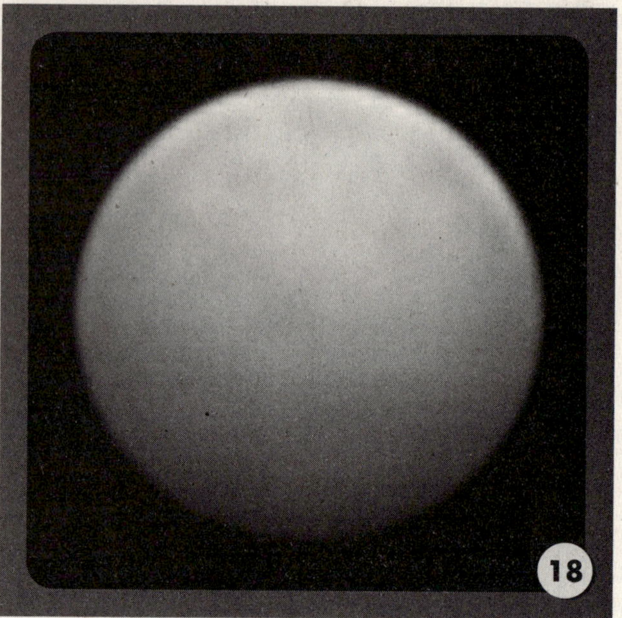

**Card #18**
Pluto

**Card #19**
chick in nest

**Card #20**
hermit crab in shell



Picture Sorting Cards

# Picture Sorting Cards

**Card #21**
elf owl in cactus

**Card #22**
gray foxes in den

**Card #23**
golden retriever

**Card #24**
swan

# Picture Sorting Cards

**Card #25**
barracuda

**Card #26**
alligator

**Card #27**
tree frog

**Card #28**
lion's teeth





Picture Sorting Cards

# Picture Sorting Cards

**Card #29**
mouse's teeth

**Card #30**
alligator's teeth

**Card #31**
goat's teeth

**Card #32**
zebra's teeth

# Picture Sorting Cards

**Card #33**
shark's teeth

**Card #34**
sun

**Card #35**
marigold

**Card #36**
bee

# Picture Sorting Cards

**Card #37**
bee-eater

**Card #38**
robin eggs

**Card #39**
hatching of robin

**Card #40**
robin hatchling

# Picture Sorting Cards

**Card #41**
robin chick

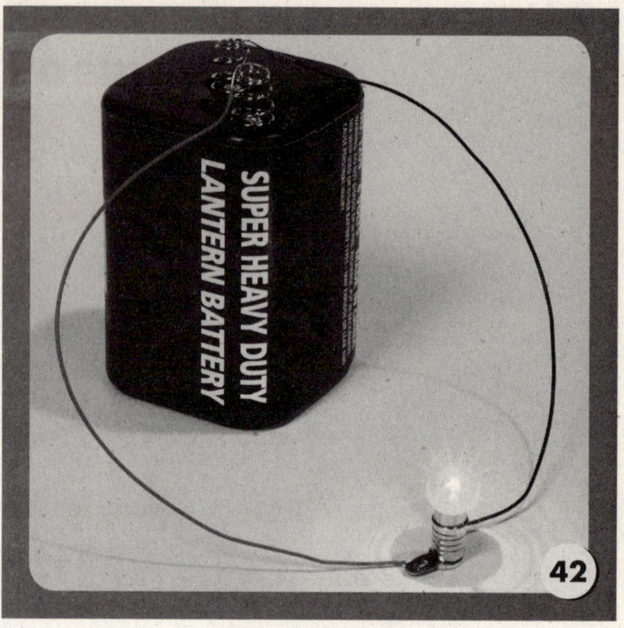


**Card #42**
closed circuit

**Card #43**
open circuit

**Card #44**
xylophone

# Picture Sorting Cards

**Card #45**
guitar strings

**Card #46**
elephant

**Card #47**
mammoth

# HURRICANE TRACKING CHART

REMEMBER, hurricanes are large and powerful storms that can suddenly change direction. Check frequently on the storm's progress until all Watches and Warnings for your area from the National Weather Service are canceled.

**HURRICANE WATCH:** hurricane may threaten within 36 hours
- Be prepared to take action if a warning is issued by the National Weather Service.
- Keep informed of the storm's progress.

**HURRICANE WARNING:** hurricane expected to strike within 24 hours
- Leave beachfront and low-lying areas.
- Leave mobile homes for more substantial shelter.
- Stay in your home if it is sturdy, on high ground, and not near the beach, but if you are asked to leave by authorities, go!
- Stay tuned to radio, NOAA Weather Radio, or television for hurricane advisories and safety information.

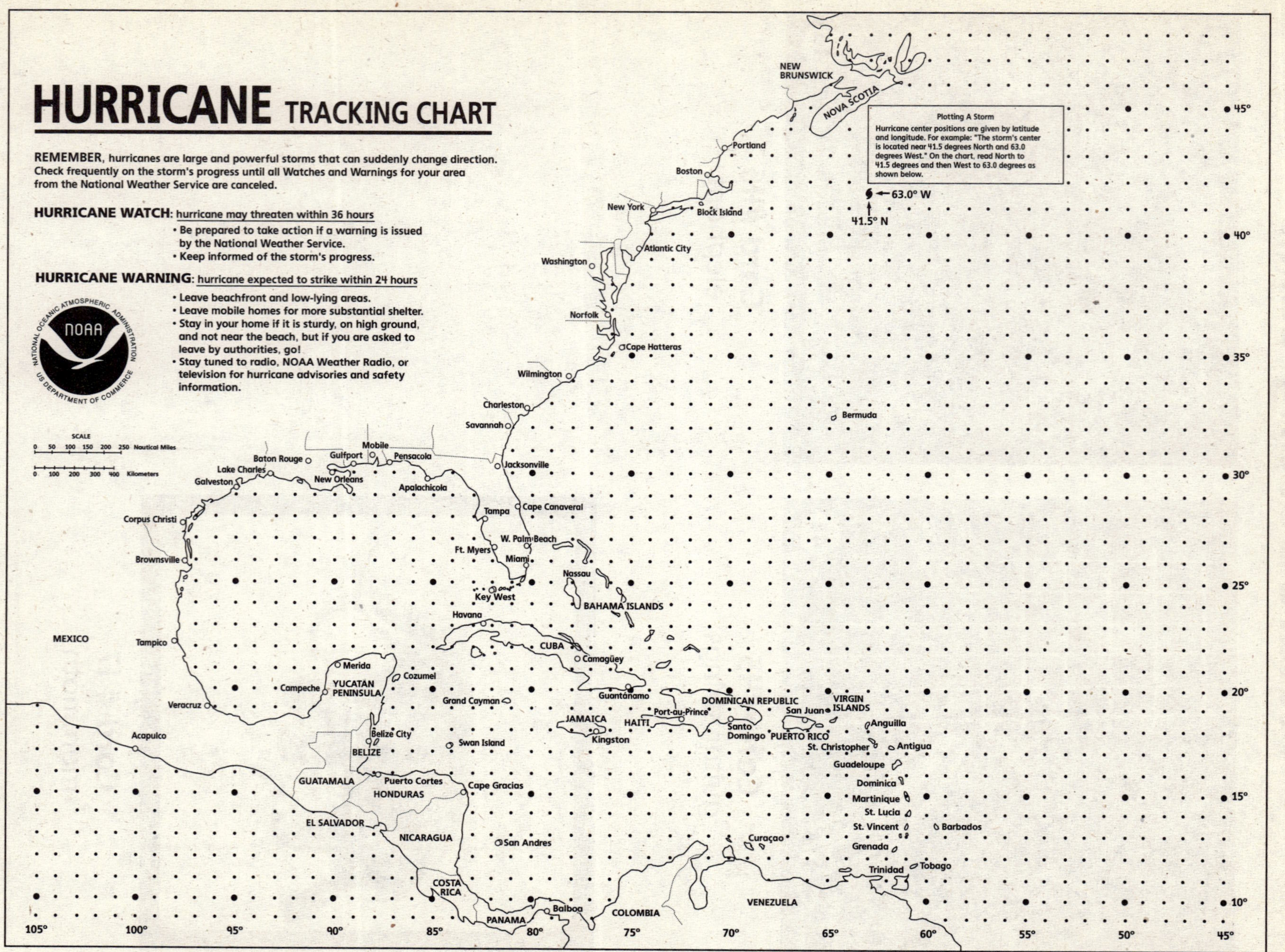


© Harcourt

# Thermometers

## Inside

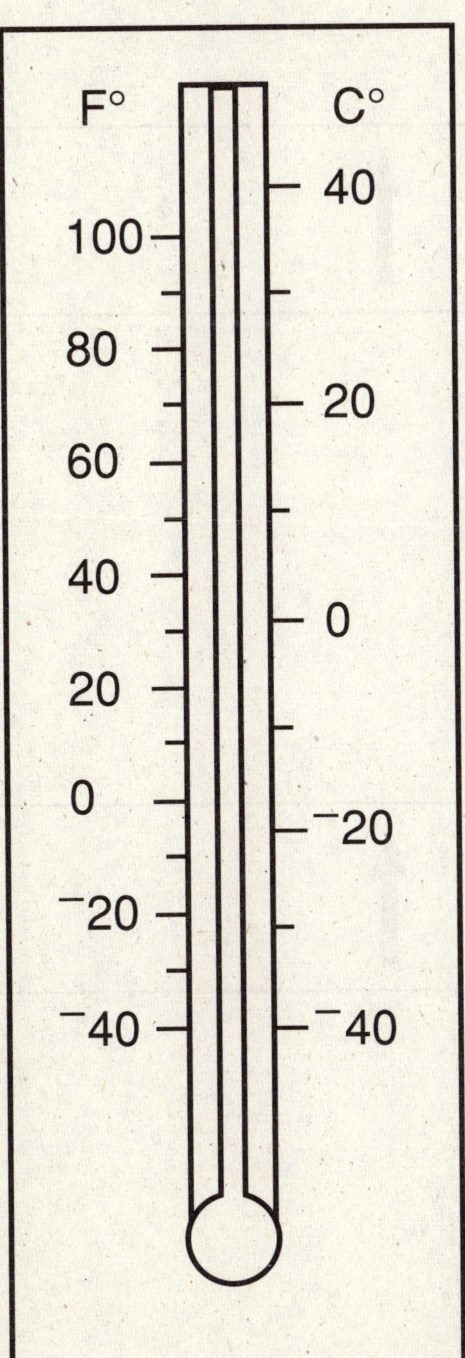



## Outside

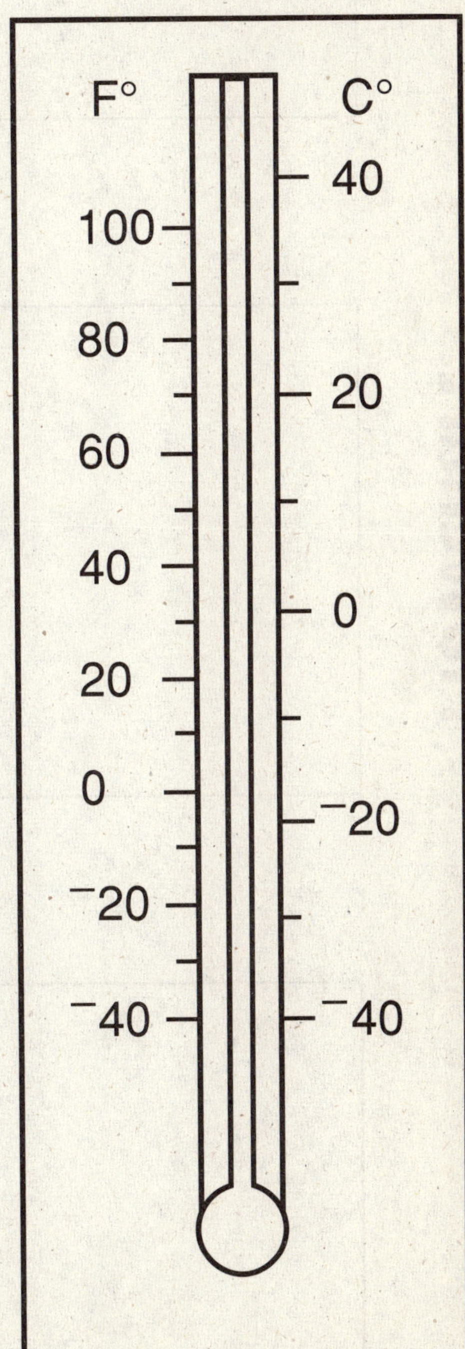

Name _______________ Date _______________

# Flowchart

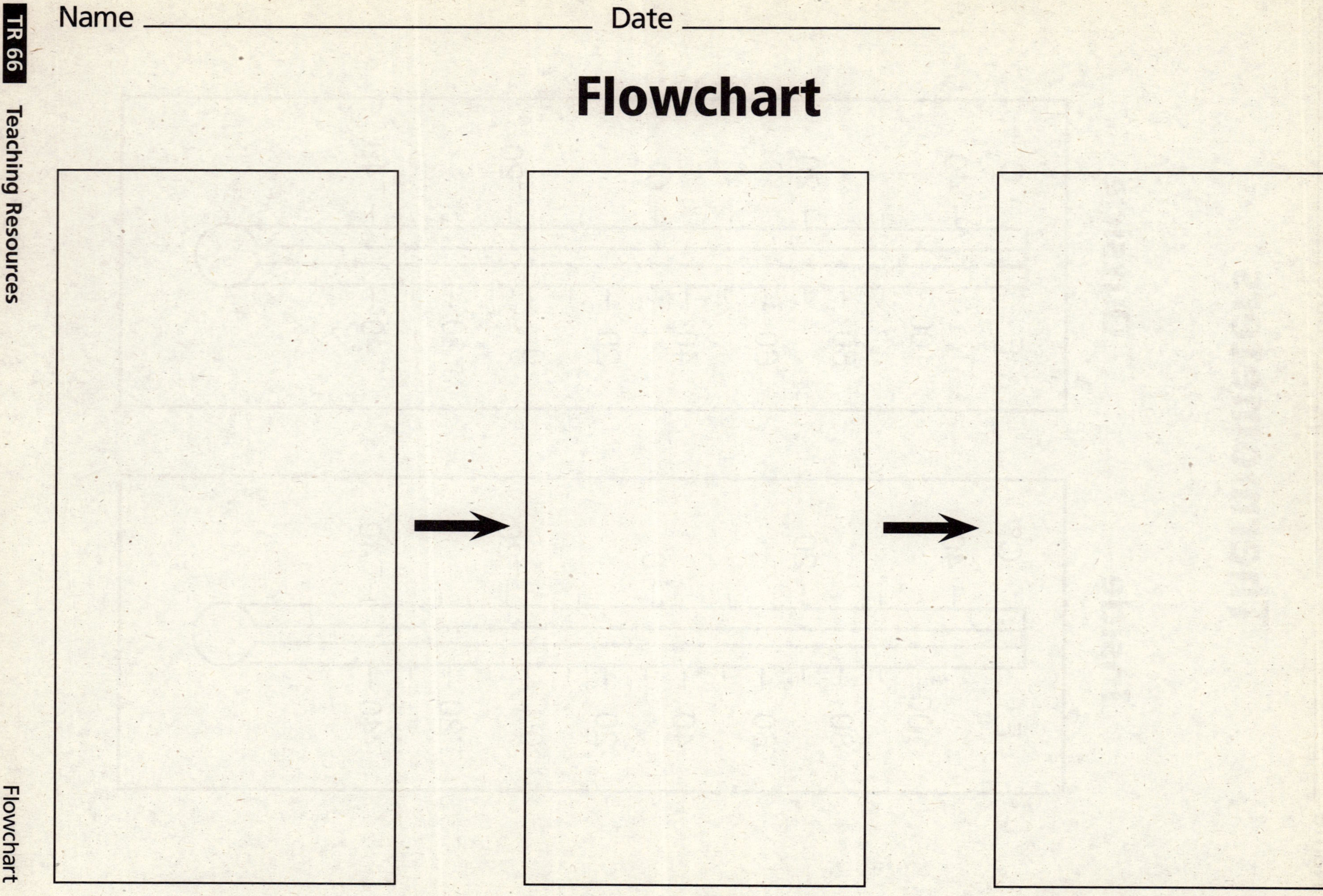

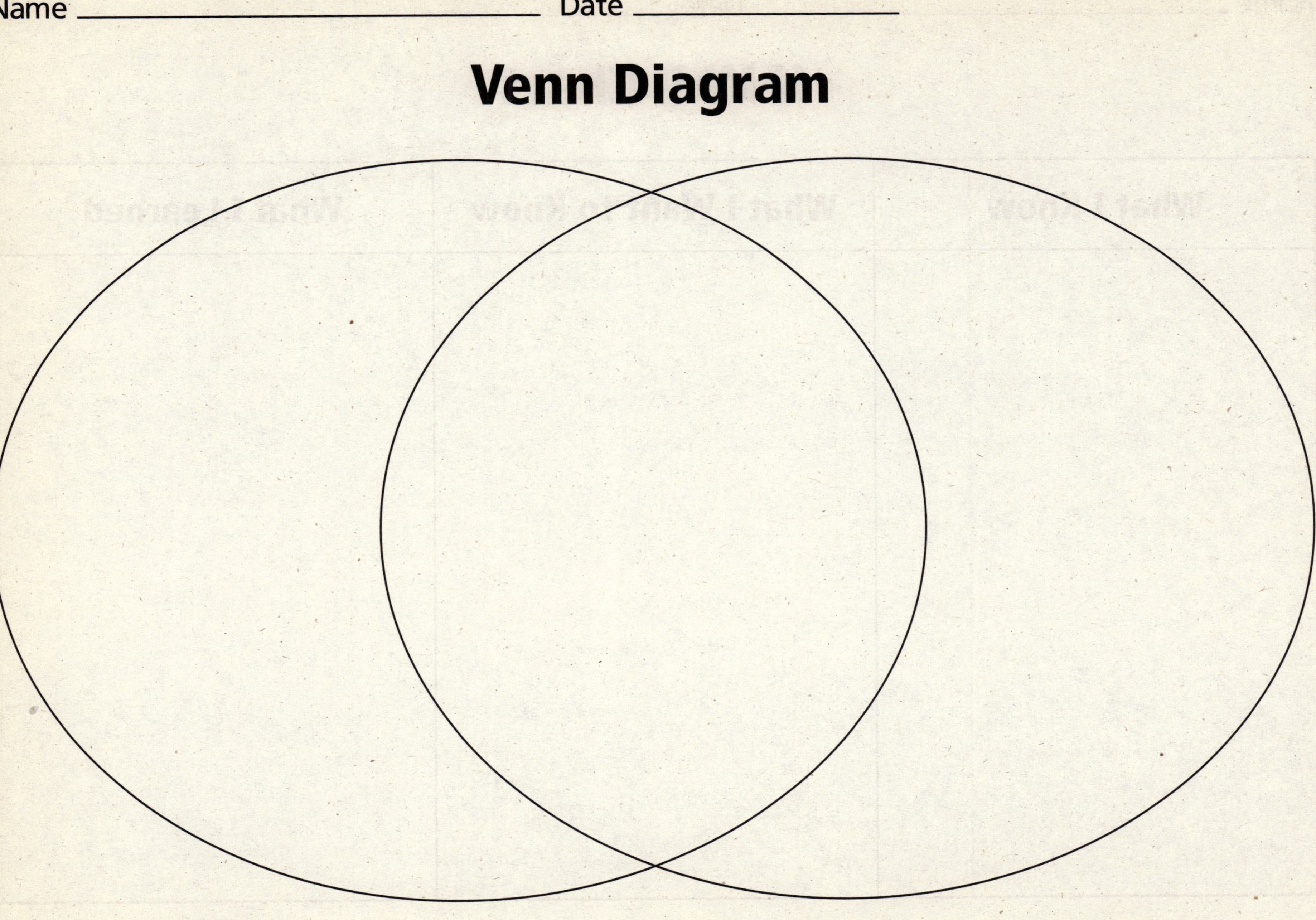



**Venn Diagram**

Name _______________________________ Date _______________________

# K-W-L Chart

| What I <u>K</u>now | What I <u>W</u>ant to Know | What I <u>L</u>earned |
| --- | --- | --- |
|  |  |  |

# Web

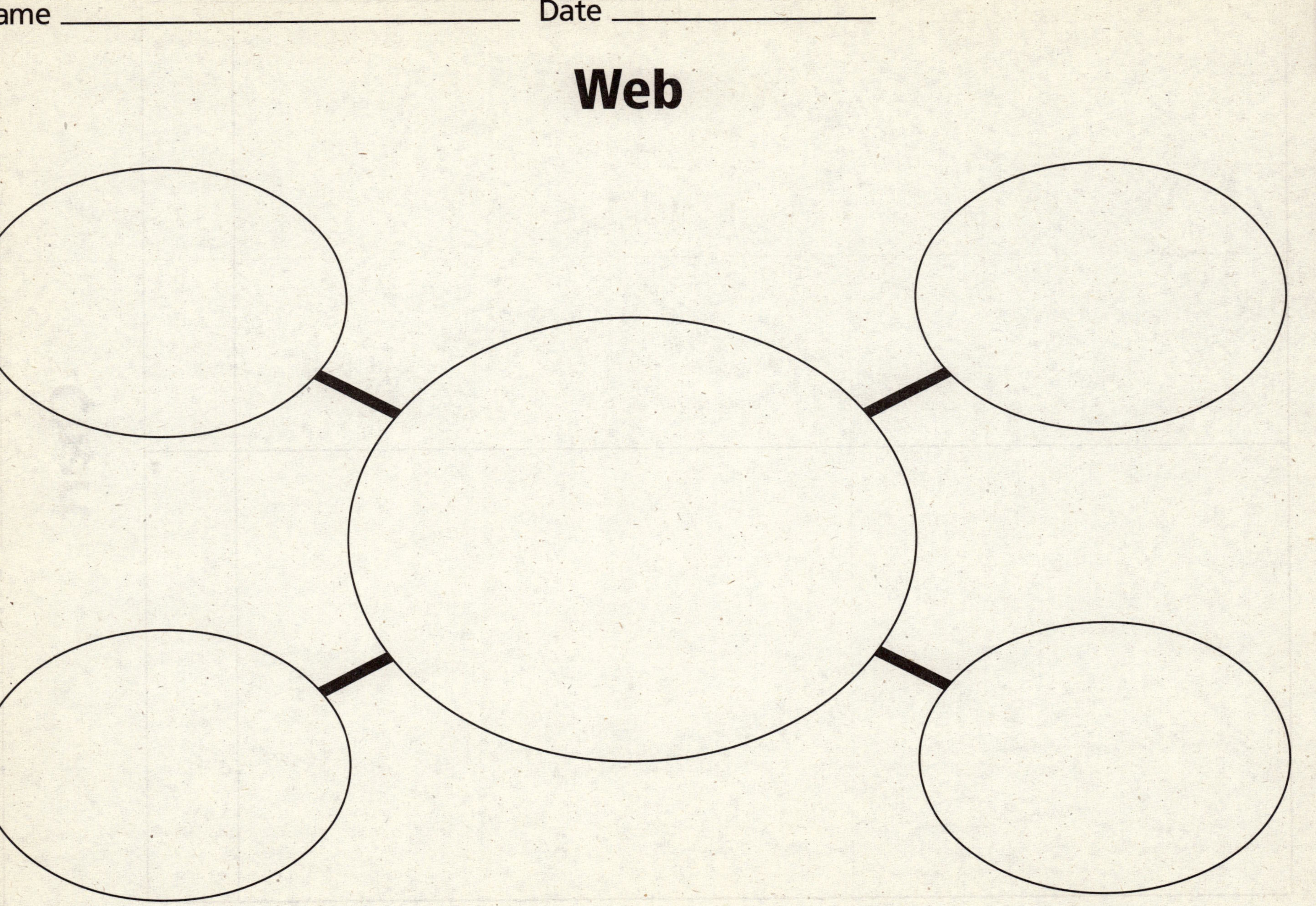

# Chart

<table>
<tr><td></td><td></td></tr>
<tr><td></td><td></td></tr>
</table>

1-inch graph grid

**Teaching Resources**   **TR 71**

1-cm graph grid

0.5-cm graph grid

# Vocabulary Activities

The activities listed here suggest ways to use word cards to do the following:

- increase students' understanding of science terms and concepts.
- help students develop their decoding (phonics and structural analysis) skills.
- meet the individual needs of your classroom.

You may wish to make your own cards, or have students make word cards, for these activities. Vocabulary picture cards for all glossary terms are provided for students in *Reading Support and Homework*.

## Concept Activities

## ① Categories

**Grouping:** Whole class or large group; pairs (Challenge)
**Materials:** word cards; paper and pencil (Challenge)

Have students work with words that are clearly related, either looking for words that fit categories, identify categories, or make categories. Here are some examples.

| Categories | Vocabulary Words |
|---|---|
| Layers of Earth | mantle, crust, core |
| Objects in Space | comet, planet, star |
| Parts of Plants | leaf, root, stem |
| Types of Rocks | igneous rock, metamorphic rock, sedimentary rock |
| Kinds of Animals, Living Things | amphibian, mammal, reptile |
| Landforms | canyon, plateau, valley |
| Forms of Matter | liquid, gas, solid |

**Easy:** Give students the category and help them search through the word cards to find words that fit.

**Average:** Give students three vocabulary words and have them decide what category best describes all three.

**Challenge:** Have student partners identify their own sets of word cards and categories. Provide time for partners to challenge other pairs to match words and categories. Give them the option of adding a non vocabulary word to fill out a category.

# ② Antonym Antics

**Grouping:** Whole class or large group
**Materials:** word cards; drawing materials
(Easy and Challenge)

Before beginning the activity, separate pairs of antonyms from the word cards. Start by discussing what antonyms are (words with opposite meanings), using common opposites such as *hard* and *easy*, *tall* and *short*, *day* and *night*.

**Easy:** Display pairs of antonyms. Discuss how the two words in each set differ in meaning. Then have students choose a pair to illustrate, showing in the drawing how opposite the words are in meaning. Ask students to share their drawings.

**Average:** Add 6 word cards to the deck as distracters. Then select a word card that has an opposite and talk about the word's meaning. Have students find a word that is an antonym. Discuss how these two words differ.

**Challenge:** Have students look through the word cards for a word that they can name an antonym for. Tell them that they can match up word cards or match a word card with a word they know. Ask students to write a description for each set of opposites without using either word. Have them exchange descriptions with a partner and challenge the partner to identify the words described.

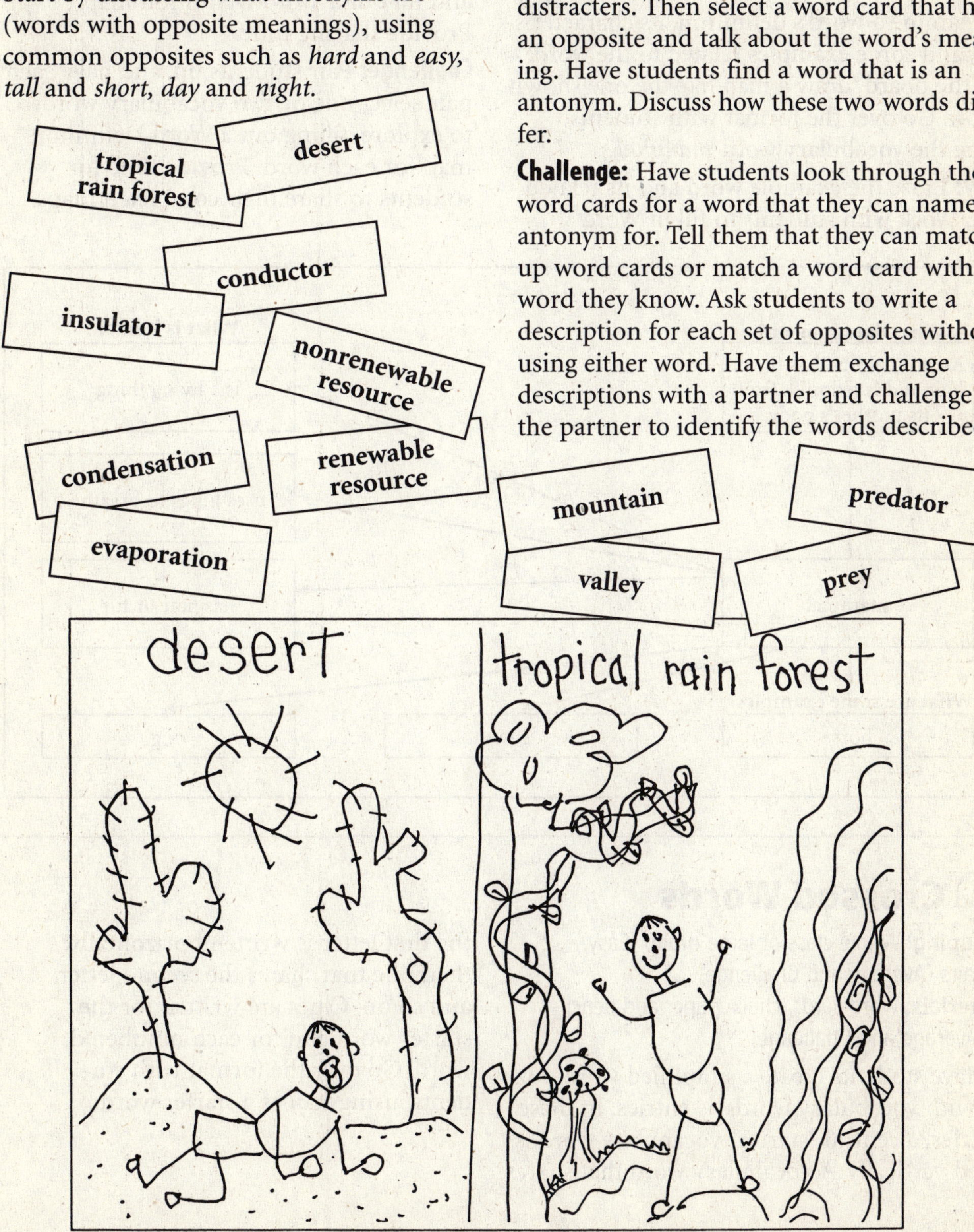

# ③ Word Definition Map

**Grouping:** Whole class or large group; small group (Average); pairs (Challenge)

**Materials:** word cards, chalk; paper and pencil (Average and Challenge)

Have students explore certain words in depth. Have them use a Word Definition Map to examine a word's definition, its characteristics, and some examples related to the word. On the board, draw a map like the one shown below. Go over the format with students, using the vocabulary word *mammal*.

**Easy:** Erase the example word and its related text. Work with students to fill in Word Definition maps for one or two of these words: *amphibian, reptile, constellation, forest, planet, rock.*

**Average:** Divide students into small groups. List these words on the board: *amphibian, reptile, constellation, forest, planet, rock.* Have each group pick a word and fill out a Word Definition map. Provide sharing time.

**Challenge:** Pair students up, and have each pair select one or two vocabulary words to explore, filling out a Word Definition map for each word. Provide time for students to share their completed maps.

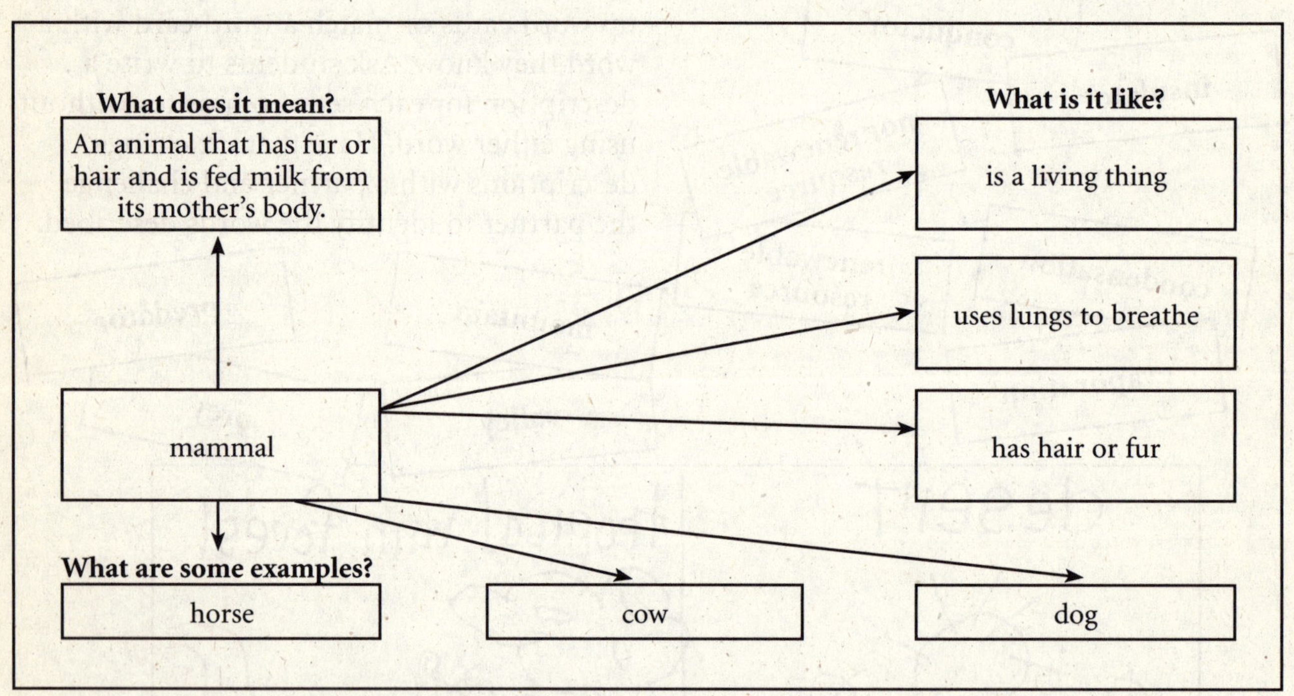


# ④ Crossed Words

**Grouping:** Whole class or large group (Easy), Pairs (Average and Challenge)

**Materials:** word cards, chalk, paper and pencil (Average and Challenge)

Have students create a simplified word puzzle with vocabulary words as entries. In these puzzles, a central "starter" vocabulary word is listed vertically. A vocabulary word that shares the first letter is written horizontally, then one that shares the second letter, and so on. Clues are written for the starter word and for each numbered word. Go over the format with students, using *root* as a starter word.

**Starter Word Clue:** What is the part of a plant that is under the ground?

1. | o | **r** | b | i | t |
2. | **c** | **o** | **r** | e |
3. | f | l | **o** | o | d |
4. | **h** | e | a | **t** |

1. path of a planet as it revolves around the sun
2. center of Earth
3. great flow of water over land
4. transfer of thermal energy from a piece of matter to another

**Easy:** Work with students to create a crossed words puzzle on the board. Help them look through their word cards for a good four- or five-letter starter word, let them find words that share common letters, and work with them to create clues.

**Average:** Have students work in small groups to make their own puzzle, using a four- or five-letter starter word of their choice.

**Challenge:** Have students work in small groups to make their own puzzle. Tell them to select a longer vocabulary word, such as *germinate*, to be the starter word.

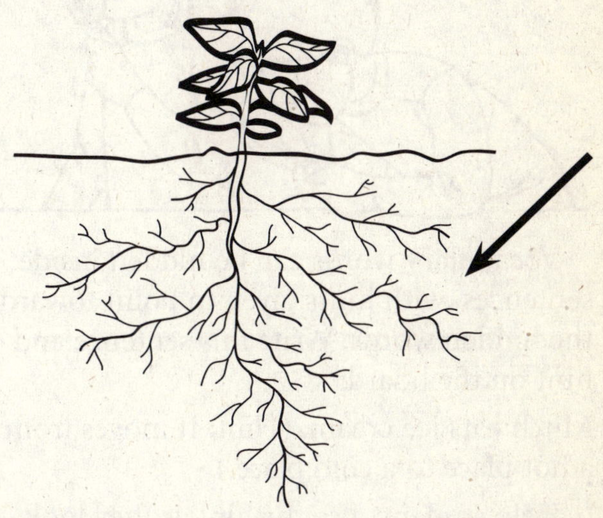

---

# ⑤ Mixed Meanings

**Grouping:** Whole class or large group (Easy), small group (Average and Challenge)

**Materials:** word cards, chalk, *Science* glossary, dictionary; paper and pencil (Average and Challenge)

Have students work with words that have meanings other than their glossary definitions. Use the word *star* as an example, contrasting the glossary definition ("a hot ball of glowing gases") with the concept of a movie star. List these vocabulary words on the board: *conductor, plain, rock, root, scales, stem.*

**Easy:** For each word, have students find and dictate the glossary definition. Write it on the board. Ask students to give any other meanings they know for the word. Then have them take turns finding the word in the dictionary and reading out other definitions. Help them pick a contrasting definition, and write it on the board. Have students suggest context sentences for each meaning of the word.

**Average:** Have students work in small groups, writing down the glossary definition of a word, finding a contrasting dictionary definition, and coming up with context sentences. Give them a chance to share their work.

**Challenge:** Use the procedure described in "Average," but challenge students to come up with a single context sentence that includes the contrasting meanings for a word. (For example: The movie <u>stars</u> looked up at the <u>stars</u>.)

# ⑥ Hidden Words

**Grouping:** Whole class or large group (Easy), small group (Average), pairs (Challenge)

**Materials:** word cards, chalk; paper and pencil (Average and Challenge)

Vocabulary words can be hidden inside sentences, with hints given to point toward the hidden words. Write this sentence and hint on the board:

Mitch eats ice cream. (Hint: It moves from a hot place to a cold place.)

Help students use the hint as they look through their word cards to find the word *heat*. Underline it (Mit<u>ch eat</u>s).

**Easy:** Write the following sentences and hints on the board. Work with students to find the hidden words *fish, gas, soil,* and *star.*
- Jeff is happy near the beach. (Hint: It swims and has scales.)
- Keep the water boiling as you cook. (Hint: It's a form of matter, like air.)
- I'm so ill that I can't help in the garden. (Hint: Plants grow in this.)
- She lost a ring on that dark night. (Hint: It's a bright object in the night sky.)

**Average:** Have students work in small groups to come up with sentences and hints for the words *fish, gas, soil,* and *star.*

**Challenge:** Have students work in pairs, looking through the word cards for 2–4 words to hide in sentences. They can then exchange papers with their partners to find one another's hidden words.

---

## Decoding Activities

# ⑦ Sorting Center

**Grouping:** Individual or pairs

**Materials:** word cards, index cards, crayons or colored markers

Give students a set of word cards to sort. Explain that they need to listen to the sounds in the word on each card to sort them. Tailor the number of cards and the sorting task to their abilities, as described below.

**Easy:** On each of three index cards, have students draw and label a picture of an animal whose name ends with a target consonant sound, such as *deer, lio<u>n</u>,* or *sea<u>l</u>.* Then give students 6–8 cards with words that end with one of those 3 sounds. Have them sort the cards by ending sounds, placing each card under the appropriate animal.

**Average:** Give students 8–10 cards with one-syllable words. Ask them to sort the cards into groups that contain the same vowel sounds. You might model identifying two cards that contain matching vowel sounds, such as *speed* and *heat.*

Vocabulary Activities

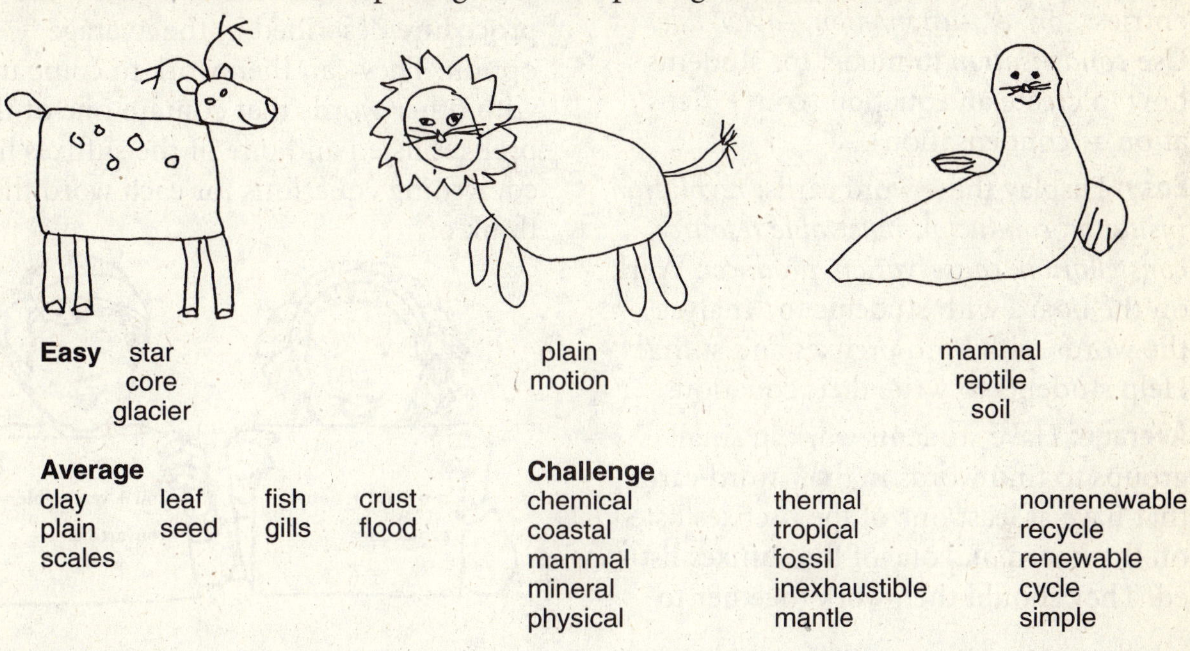

**Easy**    star          plain          mammal
        core          motion        reptile
        glacier                     soil

| **Average** | | | | **Challenge** | | |
|---|---|---|---|---|---|---|
| clay | leaf | fish | crust | chemical | thermal | nonrenewable |
| plain | seed | gills | flood | coastal | tropical | recycle |
| scales | | | | mammal | fossil | renewable |
| | | | | mineral | inexhaustible | cycle |
| | | | | physical | mantle | simple |

---

# ⑧ Syllable Sort

**Grouping:** Large or small group
**Materials:** word cards, access to a dictionary

Have students play a card game in which they collect words according to the number of syllables they hear. Have student partners deal 6–8 word cards and put the remaining words in a pile face down. Tell them to take turns choosing a card from the top of the deck, and deciding whether to keep or discard it. For example, a player collecting two-syllable words would discard a one- or three-syllable word. Discarded cards should be placed face up in a pile. The next player can choose from the word card deck or from the top of the discard pile.

The game ends when one player or the other has a complete set of words with the same number of syllables.

**Easy:** Limit the activity to 1- and 2-syllable words. Have pairs of students practice clapping out the number of syllables in some familiar words *(book, ruler, pencil, chalk)* before they begin sorting the word cards.

**Average:** Give students a chance to review the word cards before the game begins. If they are not sure how many syllables are in a word (such as *temperature*), they should consult a glossary or dictionary.

**Challenge:** Limit the activity to 3- and 4-syllable words. You may wish to provide time for students to review the vocabulary words before they begin the game.

# ⑨ Word Equations

**Grouping:** Whole class or large group (Easy), small group (Average and Challenge)
**Materials:** chalk; paper and pencil (Average and Challenge)

Students can use structural analysis to chunk multisyllabic words, creating "equations" that consist of the following: prefix(es) + root word + suffix = word.

Write the equation on the board and review it with students. To the side, write *Prefixes* and list *con-, ex-/e-, in-, pro-,* and *re-*. Then write *Suffixes* and list three entries: *-or/-er, -ation/-tion, -able/-ible*. Use *condensation* to model for students how to create an equation (con + dens + ation = condensation).

**Easy:** Display these word cards: *revolution, insulator, conductor, renewable resource, constellation, conservation, producer.* Work on the board with students to "analyze" the words with both prefixes and suffixes. Help students to write their equations.

**Average:** Have students work in small groups to find words in their word cards that have at least one of the prefixes listed on the board *and* one of the suffixes listed. They should then work together to write equations for these words. Provide time for groups to share and compare their work.

**Challenge:** Students should follow the procedure described in the Average option. They can then work to come up with other words that contain one of the prefixes listed and one of the suffixes listed, writing equations for each word they think of.

# ⑩ Rhyme Time Match

**Grouping:** Whole class or large group (Easy), pairs (Average and Challenge)
**Materials:** word cards, chalk; 4 × 6 index cards cut in half, pencils (Average and Challenge)

Have students work with different spellings for the same phoneme as they match up rhyming words. Display the following word cards: *bird, clay, core, flood, force, front, gas, loam, mass, prey, scales, trait, weight.*

**Easy:** Pick out the word *trait,* and help students find a word that rhymes (weight). List these two words on the board, noting the different spellings for the phoneme āt. Follow a similar procedure with *clay/prey* and *gas/mass.* For each remaining word, have students suggest rhymes; pick out and list a word that has a different spelling for the phoneme (examples: bird/word, core/roar, flood/mud, force/horse, front/hunt, scales/tails).

**Average:** Along with the displayed word cards, list these words on the board: *word, roar, mud, horse, hunt, home, tails.* Have students work in pairs, and have partners work together to write each word on a separate index card. When they are done, they should shuffle the "deck" and place the cards face down in a 4 × 5 grid. They can then play a matching game with rhyming words: Player 1 turns over two random cards. If the words rhyme, the player has made a match, takes the cards, and goes again. If not, play goes to the partner. When all the cards have been matched, the player with the most pairs wins.

**Challenge:** Have student partners come up with their own 10 rhyming pairs. Tell them that the rhyming parts of the words have to be spelled differently; use *trait/weight, prey/clay,* and *mass/gas* as examples. Then have them write on cards and play the matching game, as described in the Average option.